Assessment

 Assessing the Common Core State Standards

Send all inquiries to:
McGraw-Hill Education
Two Penn Plaza
New York, New York 10121

ISBN: 978-0-02-129952-2
MHID: 0-02-129952-6

Printed in the United States of America.

1 2 3 4 5 6 7 8 9 LKV 18 17 16 15 14 13

Bothell, WA • Chicago, IL • Columbus, OH • New York, NY

Cover: Nathan Love

www.mheonline.com/readingwonderworks

Send all inquiries to:
McGraw-Hill Education
Two Penn Plaza
New York, New York 10121

ISBN: 978-0-02-129952-2
MHID: 0-02-129952-8

Printed in the United States of America.

6 7 8 9 10 QVS 18 17 16 15

Table of Contents

Assessment

The *Assessment* BLM is an integral part of the complete assessment program aligned with the Common Core State Standards (CCSS) and the core reading and intervention curriculums of *McGraw-Hill Reading WonderWorks* and *McGraw-Hill Reading Wonders*.

Assessment focuses on key areas of English Language Arts as identified by the CCSS—phonological and phonemic awareness, phonics, and word recognition.

Purpose of *Assessment*

The instruction in *McGraw-Hill Reading WonderWorks* is parallel to the instruction in *McGraw-Hill Reading Wonders*. Children's results in *Assessment* provide a picture of achievement within *McGraw-Hill Reading WonderWorks* and a signal as to whether children can successfully transition back to Approaching Level reading instruction.

Assessment offers the opportunity to monitor progress in a steady and structured manner while providing formative assessment data.

As children complete each unit of the intervention program, they will be assessed on their understanding of key instructional content. The results of the assessments provided in Assessment can be used to inform subsequent instruction and assist with grouping and leveling designations.

Components of *Assessment*

- Unit Assessment
- Letter Naming Fluency Assessment
- Sight Word Fluency Assessment (Units 6-10)

Unit Assessment

Each Unit Assessment features 20 selected response items divided among four skill areas: phonological awareness, phonemic awareness, phonics, and high-frequency words. The number of questions asked in each category shifts mid-way through the year to reflect changing instructional emphasis as children's skills develop.

Units 1-5

- 4 items assessing Phonological Awareness
- 7 items assessing Phonemic Awareness
- 6 items assessing Phonics
- 3 items assessing High-Frequency Words

Units 6-10

- 3 items assessing Phonological Awareness
- 5 items assessing Phonemic Awareness
- 6 items assessing Phonics
- 6 items assessing High-Frequency Words

Ten Letter Naming Fluency Assessments and 5 Sight Word Fluency Assessments (for use with Units 6-10) are provided as well. Use these diagnostic assessments as needed, for additional assistance in monitoring children's progress.

Administering the Assessments

Each test should be administered at the end of each unit of instruction. Make a copy of the assessment and the Scoring Sheet for each child.

After each child has a copy of the assessment, provide a version of the following directions: Say: *Write your name on the top of each page of this assessment. (When children are finished, continue with the directions.) I will read questions to you. Listen carefully. Choose the correct answer to each question and draw a circle around it. When you have completed the assessment, put your pencil down and turn the pages over. You may begin now.*

Evaluating the Assessments

Each Unit Assessment is worth 20 points, with each item worth 1 point. A Scoring Sheet and an Answer Key are provided to help with scoring. Note children's success or difficulty with specific skills on the Scoring Sheet. Use this data to determine the instructional focus going forward. Reteach tested skills for children who score under 80%.

Transitioning into *McGraw-Hill Reading Wonders* Instruction

Moving children into Approaching Level *McGraw-Hill Reading Wonders* instruction at the completion of a unit should be guided by assessment data, children's performance during the unit instruction, and informal observation of children's progress.

Use the following assessment criteria to help judge children's readiness for Approaching Level designation and materials:

- Score of 70% or higher on *McGraw-Hill Reading Wonders* Unit Assessment

- Achieving unit Letter Naming and Sight Word Fluency Assessment goals

- Ability to read and comprehend the Reading/Writing Workshop Shared Read from *McGraw-Hill Reading Wonders*

- Mastery of the unit benchmark skills in the Foundational Skills Kit and *Reading Wonders* Adaptive Learning

Name: _____

S

  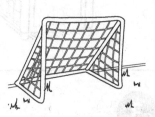

I

GO ON →

2

3

  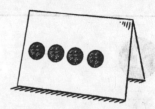

4

STOP

Name: _____

5

6 ★

7

Name: _____

8

9

 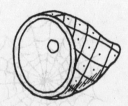 

Name: _____

10

11

 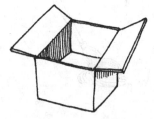 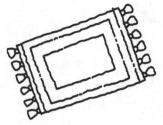

STOP

Name: _____

12
🍎

a

A **S** **D**

13
★

M

f **m** **r**

14
🌲

g **k** **m**

GO ON →

Name: _____

15

m   **d**   **h**

16

l   **a**   **s**

17

a   **n**   **w**

STOP

Name: _____

18 🍎

can   the   I

19 ★

the   can   we

20 🌲

I   we   can

STOP

Name: _____

S

l

  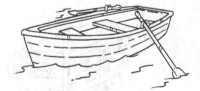

GO ON →

Name: _____

2

🍎

  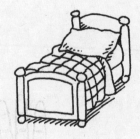

3

⭐

4

🌲

STOP

Name: _____

5

6

7

  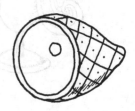

GO ON →

Name: _____

8

🍎

9

⭐

 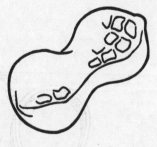 

GO ON →

Name: _____

10

11

★

STOP

Name: _____

12

pat   at   sat

13

sap   tap   map

14

mat   pat   sat

GO ON →

Name: _____

15

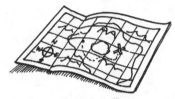

tap   sap   map

16

map   tap   sap

17

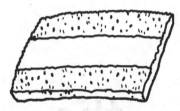

mat   pat   sat

STOP

Name: _____

18

the　　　　see　　　　a

19

a　　　　we　　　　I

20

can　　　　the　　　　like

STOP

Name: _____

GO ON →

Name: _____

2

3

4

STOP

Name: _____

5

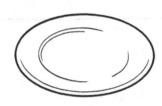

6

7

Name: _____

Name:

8

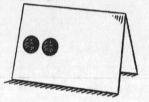  

9

Name: _____

10

  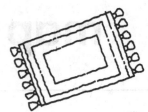

11

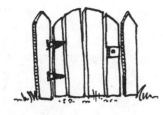  

STOP

Name: _____

12

map   sap   tap

13

sat   mat   pat

14

sap   sit   tip

Name: _____

15

pan   pin   pat

16

nap   tap   map

17

pat   pit   pan

STOP

18
🍎

| the | like | we |

19
⭐

| to | see | a |

20
🌲

| we | the | and |

STOP

Name: _____

 S

 l

GO ON →

Name: _____

2

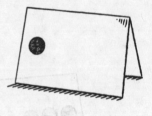  

3

4

STOP

Name: _____

5

6

★

7

   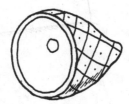   

GO ON →

Name: _____

8

9

★

  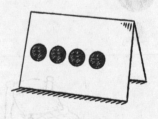

GO ON →

Name: _____

10

11

STOP

Name: _____

12

cap   tap   nap

13

pat   mat   cat

14

pit   pot   pat

GO ON →

Name: _____

15

top   tip   tap

16

not   dot   cot

17

sat   sap   sad

STOP

Name: _____

18

go   can   see

19

and   you   the

20

do   we   like

 STOP

Name: _____

S

  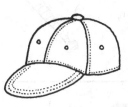

I

Name: _____

2

3 ★

4

Unit Assessment · Unit 5

Name: _____

5

6

7

GO ON →

Name: _____

8

9

★

GO ON →

Name: _____

10

 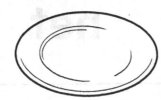 

11

STOP

Name: _____

12

pet   net   set

13

hit   hot   hat

14

top   mop   hop

GO ON →

Name: _____

15

hat   cat   pat

16

pin   pen   pan

17

tan   tin   ten

STOP

Name: _____

18

🍎

| like | and | to |

19

⭐

| the | my | go |

20

🌲

| are | do | you |

STOP

Name: _____

S

I

　　　　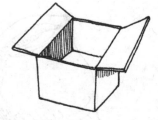

GO ON →

Name: _____

2

 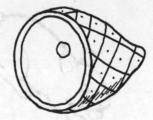 

3

STOP

Name: _____

4

5

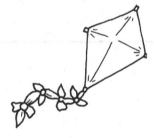  

6

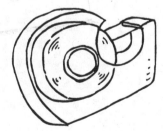  

GO ON →

Name: _____

7

🍎

 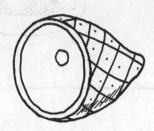 

8

⭐

STOP

Name: _____

9

fan   man   tan

10

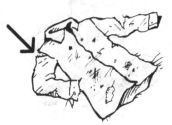

sip   tip   rip

11

bat   hat   sat

Name: _____

12

dip　　　**lip**　　　**hip**

13

pick　　　**lick**　　　**kick**

14

rock　　　**lock**　　　**sock**

STOP

　　　Unit Assessment · Unit 6

Name: _____

15

he　　　　　and　　　　　was

16

she　　　　　you　　　　　with

17

my　　　　　go　　　　　is

Name: _____

18

do   little   the

19

she   are   with

20

see   was   like

STOP

Name: _____

S

🍎

I

⭐

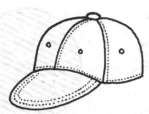  

Name: _____

2

3

 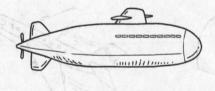 

STOP

Name: _____

4

5

6

GO ON →

7

 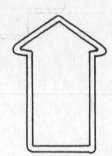 

8

STOP

Name: _____

9

bad   bed   bud

10

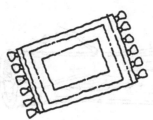

tug   bug   rug

11

kit   fit   lit

Name: _____

12

sun   fun   run

13

hog   fog   log

14

dig   wig   pig

STOP

15

they   little   my

16

was   of   she

17

with   for   you

GO ON →

Name: _____

18

🍎

like   and   have

19

⭐

are   they   see

20

🌲

of   is   to

STOP

Name: _____

S

I

  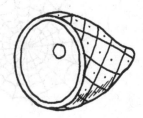

GO ON →

Name: _____

2

3

  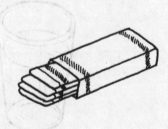

STOP

Name: _____

4

  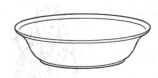

5

 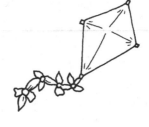 

6

GO ON →

Name: _____

7

8

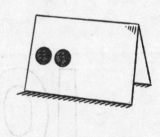  

STOP

Name: _____

9

sip   six   sit

10

net   get   vet

11

jog   hog   log

Name: _____

 12

back   tack   quack

 13

ram   yam   ham

 14

zip   dip   lip

STOP

Name: _____

15

have   said   this

16

want   are   little

17

what   they   here

Name: _____

18

me　　go　　of

19

said　　this　　my

20

here　　for　　what

 STOP

Name: _____

S

I

Name: _____

2

3

STOP

Name: _____

4

5

 ➡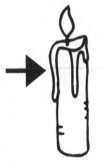

6

GO ON ➔

Name: _____

7

 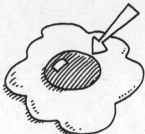 

8

 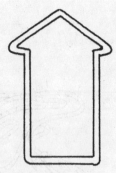 

STOP

Name: _____

9

rug   bug   jug

10

tan   van   man

11

wet   net   set

Name: _____

12

fix   six   mix

13

save   wave   gave

14

lime   time   dime

STOP

Name: _____

15

want   too   they

16

have   me   this

17

said   play   help

GO ON →

Name: _____

18

what   too   for

19

play   with   here

20

of   has   are

STOP

Name: _____

S

I

GO ON →

Name: _____

2

3

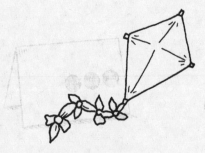  

STOP

Unit Assessment · Unit 10

Name: _____

4

 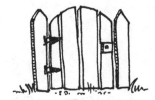 

5

6

 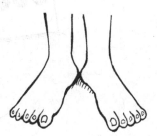 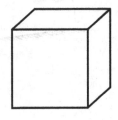

GO ON →

Name: _____

7

  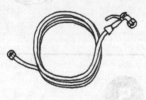

8

STOP

Name: _____

9

pole   pile   pale

10

cone   cane   cute

11

mile   mule   mole

Name: _____

12

tube　　tide　　tape

13

poke　　pike　　peek

14

wide　　weed　　wade

Name: _____

15

good   she   where

16

want   look   come

17

who   and   does

Name: _____

18

for   good   who

19

where   little   come

20

does   help   look

 STOP

Grade K Unit 1 Assessment Teacher Script

Teacher reads all directions, items, and answer choices aloud.

Phonological Awareness

Turn to page 1, the page with a picture of an alligator on it.

Check to see that all the children are on the correct page.

S *Point to the apple. I will say a word:* goat. *Now listen to these words:* boat, bat, goal. *Which word rhymes with* goat? *Listen to the words again:* boat, bat, goal. *Circle the picture whose name rhymes with* goat. *What is the answer?* **(Have a child provide the answer.)** *Yes, the word* boat *rhymes with the word* goat. *They have the same ending sounds.*

1 *Put your finger on the star under the number 1. I will say a word:* lap. *Now listen to these words:* pen, cap, tub. *Which word rhymes with* lap? *Listen to the words again:* pen, cap, tub. *Circle the picture whose name rhymes with* lap.

Turn to page 2, the page with a picture of a rabbit on it.

Check to see that all the children are on the correct page.

2 *Put your finger on the apple under the number 2. I will say a word:* red. *Now listen to these words:* bed, sock, pig. *Which word rhymes with* red? *Listen to the words again:* bed, sock, pig. *Circle the picture whose name rhymes with* red.

3 *Put your finger on the star under the number 3. I will say a sentence:* I can swim. *How many words do you hear in the sentence? Listen again:* I can swim. *Circle the picture that shows how many words you hear in the sentence,* I can swim.

4 *Put your finger on the tree under the number 4. I will say a word:* luck. *Now listen to these words:* bag, six, duck. *Which word rhymes with* luck? *Listen to the words again:* bag, six, duck. *Circle the picture whose name rhymes with* luck.

Turn to page 3, the page with a picture of a cat on it.

Check to see that all the children are on the correct page.

5 *Put your finger on the apple under the number 5. I will say a sentence:* We laugh. *How many words do you hear in the sentence? Listen again:* We laugh. *Circle the picture that shows how many words you hear in the sentence,* We laugh.

6 *Put your finger on the star under the number 6. I will say a sentence:* The horse can run. *How many words do you hear in the sentence? Listen again:* The horse can run. *Circle the picture that shows how many words you hear in the sentence,* The horse can run.

7 *Put your finger on the tree under the number 7. I will say a word:* hop. *Now listen to these words:* top, web, can. *Which word rhymes with* hop? *Listen to the words again:* top, web, can. *Circle the picture whose name rhymes with* hop.

Turn to page 4, the page with a picture of a dog on it.

Check to see that all the children are on the correct page.

8 *Put your finger on the apple under the number 8. I will say a word:* basket. *How many parts do you hear in the word* basket? *Circle the picture that shows how many parts you hear in the word* basket.

9 *Put your finger on the star under the number 9. I will say a word:* nose. *Listen to the beginning sound in* nose. /n/ /ō / /z/. *Now listen to these answer choices:* fox, ham, net. *Circle the picture whose name has the same beginning sound as* nose.

Phonemic Awareness

Turn to page 5, the page with a picture of an elephant on it.

Check to see that all the children are on the correct page.

10 *Put your finger on the apple under the number 10. I will say three words:* sad, sit, soap. *Listen for the beginning sound in each word:* /s/ /a/ /d/, /s/ /i/ /t/, /s/ /ō/ /p/. *Now listen to the answer choices:* jet, sun, log. *Circle the picture whose name has the same beginning sound you hear in* sad, sit, soap.

11 *Put your finger on the star under the number 11. I will say a word sound by sound:* /f/ /a/ /n/. *What word do you make when you blend these sounds? Listen to these answer choices:* fan, box, rug. *Circle the picture whose name you get when you blend the sounds:* /f/ /a/ /n/.

Phonics

Turn to page 6, the page with a picture of a frog on it.

Check to see that all the children are on the correct page.

12 *Put your finger on the apple under the number 12. Look at the picture. Listen to the letter name: Lowercase a.* Circle uppercase A.

13 *Put your finger on the star under the number 13. Listen to the letter name:* Capital M. *Circle lowercase* m.

14 *Put your finger on the tree under the number 14. I will say the name of the picture:* mop. *Circle the letter that stands for the sound you hear at the beginning of* mop.

Turn to page 7, the page with a picture of a goat on it.

Check to see that all the children are on the correct page.

15 *Put your finger on the apple under the number 15. I will say the name of the picture:* mouse. *Circle the letter that stands for the sound you hear at the beginning of* mouse.

16 *Put your finger on the star under the number 16. I will say the name of the picture:* ant. *Circle the letter that stands for the sound you hear at the beginning of* ant.

17 *Put your finger on the tree under the number 17. I will say the name of the picture:* apple. *Circle the letter that stands for the sound you hear at the beginning of* apple.

High-Frequency Words

Turn to page 8, the page with a picture of a horse on it.

Check to see that all the children are on the correct page.

18 *Put your finger on the apple under the number 18. Listen to this sentence:* I like pickles. *Read the answer choices. Circle the word* I.

19 *Put your finger on the star under the number 19. Listen to this sentence:* The sky is blue. *Read the answer choices. Circle the word* the.

20 *Put your finger on the tree under the number 20. Listen to this sentence:* We sit at the table. *Read the answer choices. Circle the word* we.

Grade K Unit 2 Assessment Teacher Script

Teacher reads all directions, items, and answer choices aloud.

Phonological Awareness

Turn to page 1, the page with a picture of an alligator on it.

Check to see that all the children are on the correct page.

5 *Point to the letter S. I will say the beginning sound and end sounds of a word: /h/ /and/. What word do you make when you blend these sounds together? Listen to these answer choices:* hand, heart, hat. *Circle the picture whose name blends the beginning and end sounds /h/ /and/. What is the answer?* (**Have a child provide the answer.**) *Yes, the first picture is of a hand. We get the word hand when we blend /h/ /and/.*

1 *Put your finger on the star under the number 1. I will say the beginning sound and end sounds of a word: /m/ /op/. What word do you make when you blend these sounds together? Listen to these answer choices:* mop, fan, boat. *Circle the picture whose name blends the beginning and end sounds /m/ /op/.*

Turn to page 2, the page with a picture of a rabbit on it.

Check to see that all the children are on the correct page.

2 *Put your finger on the apple under the number 2. I will say the beginning sound and end sounds of a word: /p/ /ig/. What word do you make when you blend these sounds together? Listen to these answer choices:* pig, cat, bed. *Circle the picture whose name blends the beginning and end sounds /p/ /ig/.*

3 *Put your finger on the star under the number 3. I will say two words:* sack, sit. *Now listen to these words:* rock, hill, sun. *Circle the picture whose name starts with the same sound as* sack *and* sit.

4 *Put your finger on the tree under the number 4. I will say two words:* deck, dish. *Now listen to these words:* bus, dog, cab. *Circle the picture whose name starts with the same sound as* deck *and* dish.

Phonemic Awareness

Turn to page 3, the page with a picture of a cat on it.

Check to see that all the children are on the correct page.

5 *Put your finger on the apple under the number 5. I will say three words:* nap, ten, tub. *Which word does not belong? Circle the picture that shows the word that does **not** belong.*

6 *Put your finger on the star under the number 6. I will say three words:* pan, sock, pin. *Which word does not belong? Circle the picture that shows the word that does **not** belong.*

7 *Put your finger on the tree under the number 7. I will say three words:* jet, hose, ham. *Which word does not belong? Circle the picture that shows the word that does **not** belong.*

Turn to page 4, the page with a picture of a dog on it.

Check to see that all the children are on the correct page.

8 *Put your finger on the apple under the number 8. I will say a word sound by sound:* /p/ /e/ /n/. *What word do you make when you blend these sounds? Listen to these answer choices:* car, fox, pen. *Circle the picture whose name you get when you blend the sounds:* /p/ /e/ /n/.

9 *Put your finger on the star under the number 9. I will say a word sound by sound:* /n/ /u/ /t/. *What word do you make when you blend these sounds? Listen to these answer choices:* wig, nut, bell. *Circle the picture whose name you get when you blend the sounds:* /n/ /u/ /t/.

Turn to page 5, the page with a picture of an elephant on it.

Check to see that all the children are on the correct page.

10 *Put your finger on the apple under the number 10. I will say a word:* sell. *Listen to the beginning sound in sell.* /s/ /e/ /l/. *Now listen to these answer choices:* mug, hop, sad. *Circle the picture whose name has the same beginning sound as* sell.

11 *Put your finger on the star under the number 11. I will say a word:* lap. *Listen to the beginning sound in lap.* /l/ /a/ /p/. *Now listen to these answer choices:* six, log, duck. *Circle the picture whose name has the same beginning sound as* lap.

Phonics

Turn to page 6, the page with a picture of a frog on it.

Check to see that all the children are on the correct page.

12 *Put your finger on the apple under the number 12. Look at the picture. I will say the name of the picture:* sat. *Circle the word that names the picture.*

13 *Put your finger on the star under the number 13. Look at the picture. I will say the name of the picture:* sap. *Circle the word that names the picture.*

14 *Put your finger on the tree under the number 14. Look at the picture. I will say the name of the picture:* pat. *Circle the word that names the picture.*

Turn to page 7, the page with a picture of a goat on it.

Check to see that all the children are on the correct page.

15 *Put your finger on the apple under the number 15. Look at the picture. I will say the name of the picture:* map. *Circle the word that names the picture.*

16 *Put your finger on the star under the number 16. Look at the picture. I will say the name of the picture:* tap. *Circle the word that names the picture.*

17 *Put your finger on the tree under the number 17. Look at the picture. I will say the name of the picture:* mat. *Circle the word that names the picture.*

High-Frequency Words

Turn to page 8, the page with a picture of a horse on it.

Check to see that all the children are on the correct page.

18 *Put your finger on the apple under the number 18. Listen to this sentence:* I <u>see</u> a star. *Read the answer choices. Circle the word* see.

19 *Put your finger on the star under the number 19. Listen to this sentence:* The boy has <u>a</u> book. *Read the answer choices. Circle the word* a.

20 *Put your finger on the tree under the number 20. Listen to this sentence:* A bird flies in <u>the</u> sky. *Read the answer choices. Circle the word* the.

Unit Assessment • Unit 2 Teacher Script

Grade K Unit 3 Assessment Teacher Script

Teacher reads all directions, items, and answer choices aloud.

Phonological Awareness

Turn to page 1, the page with a picture of an alligator on it.

Check to see that all the children are on the correct page.

s *Put your finger on the apple under the letter S. I will say a word: canyon. How many parts do you hear in the word canyon? Circle the picture that shows how many parts you hear in the word canyon. Look at the three pictures in the row. Choose the picture that shows the answer to the question and draw a circle around it. What is the answer?* **(Have a child provide the answer.)** *Yes, the second picture shows that the word canyon has two parts.*

1 *Put your finger on the star under the number 1. I will say a word: mouse. How many parts do you hear in the word mouse? Circle the picture that shows how many parts you hear in the word mouse.*

Turn to page 2, the page with a picture of a rabbit on it.

Check to see that all the children are on the correct page.

2 *Put your finger on the apple under the number 2. I will say a word: rabbit. How many parts do you hear in the word rabbit? Circle the picture that shows how many parts you hear in the word rabbit.*

3 *Put your finger on the star under the number 3. I will say a word: fill. Now listen to these words:* bag, duck, hill. *Which word rhymes with fill? Listen to the words again:* bag, duck, hill. *Circle the picture whose name rhymes with fill.*

4 *Put your finger on the tree under the number 4. I will say the beginning sound and end sounds of a word: /p/ /in/. What word do you make when you blend these sounds together? Listen to these answer choices:* six, pin, bell. *Circle the picture whose name blends the beginning and end sounds /p/ /in/.*

Phonemic Awareness

Turn to page 3, the page with a picture of a cat on it.

Check to see that all the children are on the correct page.

5 *Put your finger on the apple under the number 5. I will say a word sound by sound: /k/ /a/ /n/. What word do you make when you blend these sounds? Listen to these answer choices: can, wig, rock. Circle the picture whose name you get when you blend: /k/ /a/ /n/.*

6 *Put your finger on the star under the number 6. I will say a word sound by sound: /s/ /ō/ /p/. What word do you make when you blend these sounds? Listen to these answer choices: dish, soap, bat. Circle the picture whose name you get when you blend: /s/ /ō/ /p/.*

7 *Put your finger on the tree under the number 7. I will say a word: if. /iiifff/. How many sounds do you hear in the word if? Circle the picture that shows how many sounds are in the word if.*

Turn to page 4, the page with a picture of a dog on it.

Check to see that all the children are on the correct page.

8 *Put your finger on the apple under the number 8. I will say a word: nap. /nnnaaap/. How many sounds do you hear in the word nap? Circle the picture that shows how many sounds are in the word nap.*

9 *Put your finger on the star under the number 9. I will say three words: comb, net, nail. Listen to the sounds. Which word does not belong? Circle the picture that shows the word that does **not** belong: comb, net, nail.*

Turn to page 5, the page with a picture of an elephant on it.

Check to see that all the children are on the correct page.

10 *Put your finger on the apple under the number 10. I will say three words: chick, bib, rug. Listen to the sounds. Which word does not belong? Circle the picture that shows the word that does **not** belong: chick, bib, rug.*

11 *Put your finger on the star under the number 11. I will say a word: sing. Listen to the beginning sound in sing. /s/ /i/ /ng/. Now listen to these answer choices: gate, seal, bike. Circle the picture whose name has the same beginning sound as sing.*

Phonics

Turn to page 6, the page with a picture of a frog on it.

Check to see that all the children are on the correct page.

12 *Put your finger on the apple under the number 12. Look at the picture. I will say the name of the picture:* map. *Circle the word that names the picture.*

13 *Put your finger on the star under the number 13. Look at the picture. I will say the name of the picture:* pat. *Circle the word that names the picture.*

14 *Put your finger on the tree under the number 14. Look at the picture. I will say the name of the picture:* sit. *Circle the word that names the picture.*

Turn to page 7, the page with a picture of a goat on it.

Check to see that all the children are on the correct page.

15 *Put your finger on the apple under the number 15. Look at the picture. I will say the name of the picture:* pin. *Circle the word that names the picture.*

16 *Put your finger on the star under the number 16. Look at the picture. I will say the name of the picture:* nap. *Circle the word that names the picture.*

17 *Put your finger on the tree under the number 17. Look at the picture. I will say the name of the picture:* pan. *Circle the word that names the picture.*

High-Frequency Words

Turn to page 8, the page with a picture of a horse on it.

Check to see that all the children are on the correct page.

18 *Put your finger on the apple under the number 18. Listen to this sentence:* I <u>like</u> lemonade. *Read the answer choices. Circle the word* like.

19 *Put your finger on the star under the number 19. Listen to this sentence:* Mom will go <u>to</u> work. *Read the answer choices. Circle the word* to.

20 *Put your finger on the tree under the number 20. Listen to this sentence:* He can run <u>and</u> play. *Read the answer choices. Circle the word* and.

Grade K Unit 4 Assessment Teacher Script

Teacher reads all directions, items, and answer choices aloud.

Phonological Awareness

Turn to page 1, the page with a picture of an alligator on it.

Check to see that all the children are on the correct page.

S *Put your finger on the apple under the letter S. I will say a word:* butter. *How many parts do you hear in the word* butter? *Circle the picture that shows how many parts you hear in the word* butter. *Look at the three pictures in the row. Choose the picture that shows the answer to the question and draw a circle around it. What is the answer?* (**Have a child provide the answer.**) *Yes, the second picture shows that the word* butter *has two parts.*

1 *Put your finger on the star under the number 1. I will say a word:* kitten. *How many parts do you hear in the word* kitten? *Circle the picture that shows how many parts you hear in the word* kitten.

Turn to page 2, the page with a picture of a rabbit on it.

Check to see that all the children are on the correct page.

2 *Put your finger on the apple under the number 2. I will say a word:* own. *How many parts do you hear in the word* own? *Circle the picture that shows how many parts you hear in the word* own.

3 *Put your finger on the star under the number 3. I will say a word:* capital. *How many parts do you hear in the word* capital? *Circle the picture that shows how many parts you hear in the word* capital.

4 *Put your finger on the tree under the number 4. I will say a sentence:* The cat runs fast. *How many words do you hear in the sentence? Listen again:* The cat runs fast. *Circle the picture that shows how many words you hear in the sentence,* The cat runs fast.

Phonemic Awareness

Turn to page 3, the page with a picture of a cat on it.

Check to see that all the children are on the correct page.

5 *Put your finger on the apple under the number 5. I will say a word:* dime. *Listen to the beginning sound in* dime. /d/ /ī/ /m/. *Now listen to these answer choices:* lock, sun, deer. *Circle the picture whose name has the same beginning sound as* dime.

6 *Put your finger on the star under the number 6. I will say a word:* sock. *Listen to the middle sound in* sock. /s/ /o/ /k/. *Now listen to these answer choices:* mop, jet, bug. *Circle the picture whose name has the same middle sound as* sock.

7 *Put your finger on the tree under the number 7. I will say a word sound by sound:* /f/ /o/ /k/ /s/. *What word do you make when you blend these sounds? Listen to these answer choices:* bed, ham, fox. *Circle the picture whose name you get when you blend:* /f/ /o/ /k/ /s/.

Turn to page 4, the page with a picture of a dog on it.

Check to see that all the children are on the correct page.

8 *Put your finger on the apple under the number 8. I will say a word sound by sound:* /k/ /ā/ /k/. *What word do you make when you blend these sounds? Listen to these answer choices:* leaf, cake, hose. *Circle the picture whose name you get when you blend:* /k/ /ā/ /k/.

9 *Put your finger on the star under the number 9. I will say a word:* dough. /dōō̄/. *How many sounds do you hear in the word* dough? *Circle the picture that shows how many sounds are in the word* dough.

Turn to page 5, the page with a picture of an elephant on it.

Check to see that all the children are on the correct page.

10 *Put your finger on the apple under the number 10. I will say a word:* deep. /dēēēp/. *How many sounds do you hear in the word* deep? *Circle the picture that shows how many sounds are in the word* deep.

11 *Put your finger on the star under the number 11. I will say three words:* tub, ten, pig. *Which word does not belong? Circle the picture that shows the word that does **not** belong.*

Phonics

Turn to page 6, the page with a picture of a frog on it.

Check to see that all the children are on the correct page.

12 *Put your finger on the apple under the number 12. Look at the picture. I will say the name of the picture:* cap. *Circle the word that names the picture.*

13 *Put your finger on the star under the number 13. Look at the picture. I will say the name of the picture:* cat. *Circle the word that names the picture.*

14 *Put your finger on the tree under the number 14. Look at the picture. I will say the name of the picture:* pot. *Circle the word that names the picture.*

Turn to page 7, the page with a picture of a goat on it.

Check to see that all the children are on the correct page.

15 *Put your finger on the apple under the number 15. Look at the picture. I will say the name of the picture:* top. *Circle the word that names the picture.*

16 *Put your finger on the star under the number 16. Look at the picture. I will say the name of the picture:* dot. *Circle the word that names the picture.*

17 *Put your finger on the tree under the number 17. I will say the name of the picture:* sad. *Circle the word that names the picture.*

High-Frequency Words,

Turn to page 8, the page with a picture of a horse on it.

Check to see that all the children are on the correct page.

18 *Put your finger on the apple under the number 18. Listen to this sentence:* We <u>go</u> to school. *Read the answer choices. Circle the word* go.

19 *Put your finger on the star under the number 19. Listen to this sentence:* I will play a game with <u>you</u>. *Read the answer choices. Circle the word* you.

20 *Put your finger on the tree under the number 20. Listen to this sentence:* <u>Do</u> the children dance? *Read the answer choices. Circle the word* do.

Grade K Unit 5 Assessment Teacher Script

Teacher reads all directions, items, and answer choices aloud.

Phonological Awareness

Turn to page 1, the page with a picture of an alligator on it.

Check to see that all the children are on the correct page.

S *Put your finger on the apple under the letter S. I will say three words:* lip, hip, cap. *Listen to the words again:* lip, hip, cap. *Circle the picture whose name doesn't rhyme. Look at the three pictures in the row. Choose the picture that shows the answer to the question and draw a circle around it. What is the answer?* **(Have a child provide the answer.)** *Yes,* cap *does not rhyme with* lip *and* hip.

1 *Put your finger on the star under the number 1. I will say three words:* shell, cup, bell. *Listen to the words again:* shell, cup, bell. *Circle the picture whose name does* **not** *rhyme.*

Turn to page 2, the page with a picture of a rabbit on it.

Check to see that all the children are on the correct page.

2 *Put your finger on the apple under the number 2. I will say three words:* bat, fin, pin. *Listen to the words again:* bat, fin, pin. *Circle the picture whose name does* **not** *rhyme.*

3 *Put your finger on the star under the number 3. I will say a word:* helper. *How many parts do you hear in the word* helper? *Circle the picture that shows how many parts you hear in the word* helper.

4 *Put your finger on the tree under the number 4. I will say the beginning sound and end sounds of a word: /w/ /eb/. What word do you make when you blend these sounds together? Listen to these answer choices:* van, gum, web. *Circle the picture whose name blends the beginning and end sounds /w/ /eb/.*

Phonemic Awareness

Turn to page 3, the page with a picture of a cat on it.

Check to see that all the children are on the correct page.

5 *Put your finger on the apple under the number 5. I will say three words:* mix, mad, met. *Listen for the beginning sound in each word: /m/ /i/ /ks/, /m/ /a/ /d/, /m/ /e/ /t/. Now listen to the answer choices:* mouse, car, five. *Circle the picture whose name has the same beginning sound you hear in* mix, mad, met.

6 *Put your finger on the star under the number 6. I will say three words:* bit, zip, fix. *Listen for the middle sound in each word: /b/ /i/ /t/, /z/ /i/ /p/, /f/ /i/ /ks/. Now listen to the answer choices:* dig, rock, jam. *Circle the picture whose name has the same middle sound you hear in* bit, zip, fix.

7 *Put your finger on the tree under the number 7. I will say a word sound by sound: /b/ /e/ /d/. What word do you make when you blend these sounds? Listen to these answer choices:* hill, dog, bed. *Circle the picture whose name you get when you blend: /b/ /e/ /d/.*

Turn to page 4, the page with a picture of a dog on it.

Check to see that all the children are on the correct page.

8 *Put your finger on the apple under the number 8. I will say a word sound by sound: /h/ /ī/ /v/. What word do you make when you blend these sounds? Listen to these answer choices:* game, hive, rose. *Circle the picture whose name you get when you blend /h/ /ī/ /v/.*

9 *Put your finger on the star under the number 9. I will say a word:* end. /eeend/. *How many sounds do you hear in the word* end? *Circle the picture that shows how many sounds are in the word* end.

Turn to page 5, the page with a picture of an elephant on it.

Check to see that all the children are on the correct page.

10 *Put your finger on the apple under the number 10. I will say a word:* nap. *Listen to the beginning sound in* nap. /n/ /a/ /p/. *Now listen to these answer choices:* nest, dish, cub. *Circle the picture whose name has the same beginning sound as* nap.

11 *Put your finger on the star under the number 11. I will say three words:* jet, hen, box. *Which word does not belong? Circle the picture that shows the word that does **not** belong.*

Education. Permission is granted to reproduce for classroom use.

Copyright © McGraw-Hill

Phonics,

Turn to page 6, the page with a picture of a frog on it.

Check to see that all the children are on the correct page.

12 *Put your finger on the apple under the number 12. Look at the picture. I will say the name of the picture:* net. *Circle the word that names the picture.*

13 *Put your finger on the star under the number 13. Look at the picture. I will say the name of the picture:* hit. *Circle the word that names the picture.*

14 *Put your finger on the tree under the number 14. Look at the picture. I will say the name of the picture:* hop. *Circle the word that names the picture.*

Turn to page 7, the page with a picture of a goat on it.

Check to see that all the children are on the correct page.

15 *Put your finger on the apple under the number 15. Look at the picture. I will say the name of the picture:* hat. *Circle the word that names the picture.*

16 *Put your finger on the star under the number 16. Look at the picture. I will say the name of the picture:* pen. *Circle the word that names the picture.*

17 *Put your finger on the tree under the number 17. Look at the picture. I will say the name of the picture:* ten. *Circle the word that names the picture.*

High-Frequency Words

Turn to page 8, the page with a picture of a horse on it.

Check to see that all the children are on the correct page.

18 *Put your finger on the apple under the number 18. Listen to this sentence* He eats chicken <u>and</u> rice. *Read the answer choices. Circle the word* and.

19 *Put your finger on the star under the number 19. Listen to this sentence:* I eat lunch with <u>my</u> friend. *Read the answer choices. Circle the word* my.

20 *Put your finger on the tree under the number 20. Listen to this sentence:* They <u>are</u> painting their house. *Read the answer choices. Circle the word* are.

Copyright © McGraw-Hill Education. Permission is granted to reproduce for classroom use.

Grade K Unit 6 Assessment Teacher Script

Teacher reads all directions, items, and answer choices aloud.

Phonological Awareness

Turn to page 1, the page with a picture of an alligator on it.

Check to see that all the children are on the correct page.

S *Put your finger on the apple under the letter S. I will say three words:* cat, rat, dog. *Listen to the words again:* cat, rat, dog. *Circle the picture whose name does **not** rhyme. Look at the three pictures in the row. Choose the picture that shows the answer to the question and draw a circle around it. What is the answer?* (**Have a child provide the answer.**) *That's right,* dog *does not rhyme with* cat *and* rat. *It has different ending sounds.*

1 *Put your finger on the star under the number 1. I will say three words:* hen, fox, box. *Listen to the words again:* hen, fox, box. *Circle the picture whose name does **not** rhyme.*

Turn to page 2, the page with a picture of a rabbit on it.

Check to see that all the children are on the correct page.

2 *Put your finger on the apple under the number 2. I will say three words:* game, ham, ram. *Listen to the words again:* game, ham, ram. *Circle the picture whose name does **not** rhyme.*

3 *Put your finger on the star under the number 3. I will say three words:* sack, bug, tack. *Listen to the words again:* sack, bug, tack. *Circle the picture whose name does **not** rhyme.*

Phonemic Awareness

Turn to page 3, the page with a picture of a cat on it.

Check to see that all the children are on the correct page.

④ *Put your finger on the apple under the number 4. I will say a word:* bell. *Listen to the beginning sound in* bell. /b/ /e/ /l/. *Now listen to these answer choices:* sun, hat, bird. *Circle the picture whose name has the same beginning sound as* bell.

⑤ *Put your finger on the star under the number 5. I will say a word:* kid. *Listen to the beginning sound in* kid. /k/ /i/ /d/. *Now listen to these answer choices:* kite, moon, hose. *Circle the picture whose name has the same beginning sound as* kid.

⑥ *Put your finger on the tree under the number 6. I will say a word sound by sound:* /r/ /ō/ /b/. *What word do you make when you blend these sounds? Listen to these answer choices:* tape, robe, five. *Circle the picture whose name you get when you blend the sounds:* /r/ /ō/ /b/.

Turn to page 4, the page with a picture of a dog on it.

Check to see that all the children are on the correct page.

⑦ *Put your finger on the apple under the number 7. I will say a word:* egg. *Now listen to this sound:* /l/. *What word do you make if you add the* /l/ *sound to the beginning of* egg? *Listen to these answer choices:* cup, ham, leg. *Circle the picture that shows the word you make when you add the* /l/ *sound to the beginning of the word* egg.

⑧ *Put your finger on the star under the number 8. I will say a word:* duck. /duuuk/. *How many sounds do you hear in the word* duck? *Circle the picture that shows how many sounds are in the word* duck.

Phonics

Turn to page 5, the page with a picture of an elephant on it.

Check to see that all the children are on the correct page.

⑨ *Put your finger on the apple under the number 9. Look at the picture. I will say the name of the picture:* fan. *Circle the word that names the picture.*

⑩ *Put your finger on the star under the number 10. Look at the picture. I will say the name of the picture:* rip. *Circle the word that names the picture.*

⑪ *Put your finger on the tree under the number 11. Look at the picture. I will say the name of the picture:* bat. *Circle the word that names the picture.*

Turn to page 6, the page with a picture of a frog on it.

Check to see that all the children are on the correct page.

12 *Put your finger on the apple under the number 12. Look at the picture. I will say the name of the picture:* lip. *Circle the word that names the picture.*

13 *Put your finger on the star under the number 13. Look at the picture. I will say the name of the picture:* kick. *Circle the word that names the picture.*

14 *Put your finger on the tree under the number 14. Look at the picture. I will say the name of the picture:* lock. *Circle the word that names the picture.*

High-Frequency Words

Turn to page 7, the page with a picture of a goat on it.

Check to see that all the children are on the correct page.

15 *Put your finger on the apple under the number 15. Listen to this sentence:* He *is my cousin. Read the answer choices. Circle the word* he.

16 *Put your finger on the star under the number 16. Listen to this sentence:* I eat soup with *a spoon. Read the answer choices. Circle the word* with.

17 *Put your finger on the tree under the number 17. Listen to this sentence:* The Sun is *shining. Read the answer choices. Circle the word* is.

Turn to page 8, the page with a picture of a horse on it.

Check to see that all the children are on the correct page.

18 *Put your finger on the apple under the number 18. Listen to this sentence:* Here is a little *kitten. Read the answer choices. Circle the word* little.

19 *Put your finger on the star under the number 19. Listen to this sentence:* She *knows how to skate. Read the answer choices. Circle the word* she.

20 *Put your finger on the tree under the number 20. Listen to this sentence:* The book was *long. Read the answer choices. Circle the word* was.

Unit Assessment · Unit 6 Teacher Script

Grade K Unit 7 Assessment Teacher Script

Teacher reads all directions, items, and answer choices aloud.

Phonological Awareness

Turn to page 1, the page with a picture of an alligator on it.

Check to see that all the children are on the correct page.

S *Put your finger on the apple under the letter S. I will say two words:* fast, find. *Now listen to these words:* corn, tack, fish. *Circle the picture whose name starts with the same sound as* fast *and* find. *Look at the three pictures in the row. Choose the picture that shows the answer to the question and draw a circle around it. What is the answer?* **(Have a child provide the answer.)** *That's right,* fish *starts with the same sound as* fast *and* find.

1 *Put your finger on the star under the number 1. I will say two words:* warm, wind. *Now listen to these words:* cap, jet, wolf. *Circle the picture whose name starts with the same sound as* wind *and* warm.

Turn to page 2, the page with a picture of a rabbit on it.

Check to see that all the children are on the correct page.

2 *Put your finger on the apple under the number 2. I will say the beginning sound and end sounds of a word: /g/ /ōt/. What word do you make when you blend these sounds together? Listen to these answer choices:* goat, bike, pail. *Circle the picture whose name blends the beginning and end sounds /g/ /ōt/.*

3 *Put your finger on the star under the number 3. I will say three words:* cub, sub, dot. *Listen to the words again:* cub, sub, dot. *Circle the picture whose name does* **not** *rhyme.*

Phonemic Awareness

Turn to page 3, the page with a picture of a cat on it.

Check to see that all the children are on the correct page.

4 *Put your finger on the apple under the number 4. I will say three words:* fine, farm, fuzz. *Listen for the beginning sound in each word:* /f/ /ī/ /n/, /f/ /är/ /m/, /f/ /u/ /z/. *Now listen to the answer choices:* mule, four, bone. *Circle the picture whose name has the same beginning sound you hear in* fine, farm, fuzz.

5 *Put your finger on the star under the number 5. I will say a word sound by sound:* /d/ /e/ /n/. *What word do you make when you blend these sounds? Listen to these answer choices:* den, lock, map. *Circle the picture whose name you get when you blend:* /d/ /e/ /n/.

6 *Put your finger on the tree under the number 6. I will say a word:* us. *Now listen to this sound:* /b/. *What word do you make if you add the /b/ sound to the beginning of* us? *Listen to these answer choices:* man, rock, bus. *Circle the picture that shows the word you make when you add the /b/ sound to the beginning of the word* us.

Turn to page 4, the page with a picture of a dog on it.

Check to see that all the children are on the correct page.

7 *Put your finger on the apple under the number 7. I will say a word:* cup. /k/ /u/ /p/. *Take away the first sound /k/ from the word* cup. *What new word do you make? Listen to these answer choices:* egg, up, ox. *Circle the picture that shows what word is left when you take away the /k/ sound from the word* cup.

8 *Put your finger on the star under the number 8. I am going to say a word:* ten. *What new word do you make when you change the /t/ in* ten *to /h/? Listen to these answer choices:* hen, bib, nut. *Circle the picture that shows the new word you make when you change the /t/ in* ten *to /h/.*

Phonics

Turn to page 5, the page with a picture of an elephant on it.

Check to see that all the children are on the correct page.

9 *Put your finger on the apple under the number 9. Look at the picture. I will say the name of the picture:* bed. *Circle the word that names the picture.*

10 *Put your finger on the star under the number 10. Look at the picture. I will say the name of the picture:* rug. *Circle the word that names the picture.*

11 *Put your finger on the tree under the number 11. Look at the picture. I will say the name of the picture:* kit. *Circle the word that names the picture.*

Turn to page 6, the page with a picture of a frog on it.

Check to see that all the children are on the correct page.

12 *Put your finger on the apple under the number 12. Look at the picture. I will say the name of the picture:* Sun. *Circle the word that names the picture.*

13 *Put your finger on the star under the number 13. Look at the picture. I will say the name of the picture:* log. *Circle the word that names the picture.*

14 *Put your finger on the tree under the number 14. Look at the picture. I will say the name of the picture:* wig. *Circle the word that names the picture.*

High-Frequency Words

Turn to page 7, the page with a picture of a goat on it.

Check to see that all the children are on the correct page.

15 *Put your finger on the apple under the number 15. Listen to this sentence:* I walk <u>my</u> dog. *Read the answer choices. Circle the word* my.

16 *Put your finger on the star under the number 16. Listen to this sentence:* The party <u>was</u> yesterday. *Read the answer choices. Circle the word* was.

17 *Put your finger on the tree under the number 17. Listen to this sentence:* This gift is <u>for</u> Dad. *Read the answer choices. Circle the word* for.

Turn to page 8, the page with a picture of a horse on it.

Check to see that all the children are on the correct page.

18 *Put your finger on the apple under the number 18. Listen to this sentence:* We <u>have</u> a computer. *Read the answer choices. Circle the word* have.

19 *Put your finger on the star under the number 19. Listen to this sentence:* I know where <u>they</u> live. *Read the answer choices. Circle the word* they.

20 *Listen to this sentence:* The chair is made <u>of</u> wood. *Read the answer choices. Circle the word* of.

Grade K Unit 8 Assessment Teacher Script

Teacher reads all directions, items, and answer choices aloud.

Phonological Awareness

Turn to page 1, the page with a picture of an alligator on it.

Check to see that all the children are on the correct page.

(S) *Put your finger on the apple under the letter S. I will say the beginning sound and the end sounds of a word: /b/ /el/. What word do you make when you blend these sounds together? Listen to these answer choices:* bell, bat, bed. *Look at the three pictures in the row. Choose the picture that shows the answer to the question and draw a circle around it. What is the answer?* **(Have a child provide the answer.)** *That's right, when we blend /b/ with /ell/ we make the word* bell.

(1) *Put your finger on the star under the number 1. I will say the beginning sound and end sounds of a word: /j/ /am/. What word do you make when you blend these sounds together? Listen to these answer choices:* juice, jam, ham. *Circle the picture whose name blends the beginning and end sounds /j/ /am/.*

Turn to page 2, the page with a picture of a rabbit on it.

Check to see that all the children are on the correct page.

(2) *Put your finger on the apple under the number 2. I will say the beginning sound and end sounds of a word: /v/ /an/. What word do you make when you blend these sounds together? Listen to these answer choices:* van, fire, vase. *Circle the picture whose name blends the beginning and end sounds /v/ /an/.*

(3) *Put your finger on the star under the number 3. I will say a word:* quick. *Now listen to these words:* web, chick, gum. *Which word rhymes with* quick? *Listen to the words again:* web, chick, gum. *Circle the picture whose name rhymes with* quick.

Phonemic Awareness

Turn to page 3, the page with a picture of a cat on it.

Check to see that all the children are on the correct page.

(4) *Put your finger on the apple under the number 4. I will say a word:* yes. *Listen to the beginning sound in* yes. */y/ /e/ /s/. Now listen to these answer choices:* yarn, tape, bowl. *Circle the picture whose name has the same beginning sound as* yes.

(5) *Put your finger on the star under the number 5. I will say a word:* give. *Listen to the beginning sound in* give. */g/ /i/ /v/. Now listen to these answer choices:* phone, kite, game. *Circle the picture whose name has the same beginning sound as* give.

6 *Put your finger on the tree under the number 6. I will say a word sound by sound: /f/ /o/ /ks/. What word do you make when you blend these sounds? Listen to these answer choices:* bat, fox, ten. *Circle the picture whose name you get when you blend: /f/ /o/ /ks/.*

Turn to page 4, the page with a picture of a dog on it.

Check to see that all the children are on the correct page.

7 *Put your finger on the apple under the number 7. I am going to say a word:* mean. *What new word do you make when you change the /m/ in* mean *to /kw/? Listen to these answer choices:* queen, lake, vine. *Circle the picture that shows the new word you make when you change the /m/ in* mean *to /kw/.*

8 *Put your finger on the star under the number 8. I will say a word:* quack. */quack/. How many sounds do you hear in the word* quack? *Circle the picture that shows how many sounds are in the word* quack.

Phonics

Turn to page 5, the page with a picture of an elephant on it.

Check to see that all the children are on the correct page.

9 *Put your finger on the apple under the number 9. Look at the picture. I will say the name of the picture:* six. *Circle the word that names the picture.*

10 *Put your finger on the star under the number 10. Look at the picture. I will say the name of the picture:* vet. *Circle the word that names the picture.*

11 *Put your finger on the tree under the number 11. Look at the picture. I will say the name of the picture:* jog. *Circle the word that names the picture.*

Turn to page 6, the page with a picture of a frog on it.

Check to see that all the children are on the correct page.

12 *Put your finger on the apple under the number 12. Look at the picture. I will say the name of the picture:* quack. *Circle the word that names the picture.*

13 *Put your finger on the star under the number 13. Look at the picture. I will say the name of the picture:* yam. *Circle the word that names the picture.*

14 *Put your finger on the tree under the number 14. Look at the picture. I will say the name of the picture:* zip. *Circle the word that names the picture.*

High-Frequency Words

Turn to page 7, the page with a picture of a goat on it.
Check to see that all the children are on the correct page.

15 *Put your finger on the apple under the number 15. Listen to this sentence:* The teacher <u>said</u> her name. *Read the answer choices. Circle the word* said.

16 *Put your finger on the star under the number 16. Listen to this sentence:* They <u>want</u> to see a movie. *Read the answer choices. Circle the word* want.

17 *Put your finger on the tree under the number 17. Listen to this sentence:* You buy shoes <u>here</u>. *Read the answer choices. Circle the word* here.

Turn to page 8, the page with a picture of a horse on it.
Check to see that all the children are on the correct page.

18 *Put your finger on the apple under the number 18. Listen to this sentence:* Meet <u>me</u> at the park. *Read the answer choices. Circle the word* me.

19 *Put your finger on the star under the number 19. Listen to this sentence:* I found <u>this</u> paper on the floor. *Read the answer choices. Circle the word* this.

20 *Put your finger on the tree under the number 20. Listen to this sentence:* I know <u>what</u> time it is. *Read the answer choices. Circle the word* what.

Grade K Unit 9 Assessment Teacher Script

Teacher reads all directions, items, and answer choices aloud.

Phonological Awareness

Turn to page 1, the page with a picture of an alligator on it.

Check to see that all the children are on the correct page.

S *Put your finger on the apple under the letter S. I will say a word: elbow. How many parts do you hear in the word* elbow? *Circle the picture that shows how many parts you hear in the word* elbow. *Look at the three picture s in the row. Choose the picture that shows the answer to the question and draw a circle around it. What is the answer?* **(Have a child provide the answer.)** *That's right, there are two parts in the word* elbow: /el/ and /bō/.

Phonological Awareness, pages 1–2

1 *Put your finger on the star under the number 1. I will say a word:* rake. *How many parts do you hear in the word* rake? *Circle the picture that shows how many parts you hear in the word* rake.

Turn to page 2, the page with a picture of a rabbit on it.

Check to see that all the children are on the correct page.

2 *Put your finger on the apple under the number 2. I will say a word:* welcome. *How many parts do you hear in the word* welcome? *Circle the picture that shows how many parts you hear in the word* welcome.

3 *Put your finger on the star under the number 3. I will say a word:* side. *Now listen to these words:* hide, coat, lake. *Which word rhymes with* side? *Listen to the words again:* hide, coat, lake. *Circle the picture whose name rhymes with* side.

Phonemic Awareness

Turn to page 3, the page with a picture of a cat on it.

Check to see that all the children are on the correct page.

4 *Put your finger on the apple under the number 4. I will say three words: fake, page, tale. Listen for the middle sound in each word: /f/ /ā/ /k/, /p/ /ā/ /j/, /t/ /ā/ /l/. Now listen to the answer choices: robe, seed, mane. Circle the picture whose name has the same middle sound you hear in fake, page, tale.*

5 *Put your finger on the star under the number 5. I will say three words: tub, wax, duck. Which word does not belong? Circle the picture that shows the word that does **not** belong.*

6 *Put your finger on the tree under the number 6. I will say a word: ate. Now listen to this sound: /g/. What word do you make if you add the /g/ sound to the beginning of ate? Listen to these answer choices: gate, rope, pine. Circle the picture that shows the word you make when you add the /g/ sound to the beginning of the word ate.*

Turn to page 4, the page with a picture of a dog on it.

Check to see that all the children are on the correct page.

7 *Put your finger on the apple under the number 7. I will say a word sound by sound: /y/ /ō/ /k/. What word do you make when you blend these sounds? Listen to these answer choices: mule, yolk, cave. Circle the picture whose name you get when you blend the sounds: /y/ /ō/ /k/.*

8 *Put your finger on the star under the number 8. I will say a word: tax. /t/ /a/ /ks/. Take away the first sound /t/ from the word tax. What new word do you make? Listen to these answer choices: ax, up, ice. Circle the picture that shows what word is left when you take away the /t/ sound from the word tax.*

Phonics

Turn to page 5, the page with a picture of an elephant on it.

Check to see that all the children are on the correct page.

9 *Put your finger on the apple under the number 9. Look at the picture. I will say the name of the picture: jug. Circle the word that names the picture.*

10 *Put your finger on the star under the number 10. Look at the picture. I will say the name of the picture: van. Circle the word that names the picture.*

11 *Put your finger on the tree under the number 11. Look at the picture. I will say the name of the picture:* wet. *Circle the word that names the picture.*

Turn to page 6, the page with a picture of a frog on it.

Check to see that all the children are on the correct page.

12 *Put your finger on the apple under the number 12. Look at the picture. I will say the name of the picture:* mix. *Circle the word that names the picture.*

13 *Put your finger on the star under the number 13. Look at the picture. I will say the name of the picture:* wave. *Circle the word that names the picture.*

14 *Put your finger on the tree under the number 14. Look at the picture. I will say the name of the picture:* dime. *Circle the word that names the picture.*

High-Frequency Words

Turn to page 7, the page with a picture of a goat on it.

Check to see that all the children are on the correct page.

15 *Put your finger on the apple under the number 15. Listen to this sentence:* They <u>want</u> to take a trip. *Read the answer choices. Circle the word* want.

16 *Put your finger on the star under the number 16. Listen to this sentence:* My house is on <u>this</u> street. *Read the answer choices. Circle the word* this.

17 *Put your finger on the tree under the number 17. Listen to this sentence:* She will <u>help</u> to cook dinner. *Read the answer choices. Circle the word* help.

Turn to page 8, the page with a picture of a horse on it.

Check to see that all the children are on the correct page.

18 *Put your finger on the apple under the number 18. Listen to this sentence:* The boy can ride the bus, <u>too</u>. *Read the answer choices. Circle the word* too.

19 *Put your finger on the star under the number 19. Listen to this sentence:* Let's <u>play</u> a game. *Read the answer choices. Circle the word* play.

20 *Put your finger on the tree under the number 20. Listen to this sentence:* Dad <u>has</u> a blue car. *Read the answer choices. Circle the word* has.

Grade K Unit 10 Assessment Teacher Script

Teacher reads all directions, items, and answer choices aloud.

Phonological Awareness

Turn to page 1, the page with a picture of an alligator on it.

Check to see that all the children are on the correct page.

S *Put your finger on the apple under the letter S. I will say a word:* computer. *How many parts do you hear in the word* computer? *Circle the picture that shows how many parts you hear in the word* computer. *Look at the three picture s in the row. Choose the picture that shows the answer to the question and draw a circle around it. What is the answer?* (**Have a child provide the answer.**) *That's right, the word* computer *has three parts:* com-pu-ter.

1 *Put your finger on the star under the number 1. I will say a word:* cricket. *How many parts do you hear in the word* cricket? *Circle the picture that shows how many parts you hear in the word* cricket.

Turn to page 2, the page with a picture of a rabbit on it.

Check to see that all the children are on the correct page.

2 *Put your finger on the apple under the number 2. I will say a word:* fantastic. *How many parts do you hear in the word* fantastic? *Circle the picture that shows how many parts you hear in the word* fantastic.

3 *Put your finger on the star under the number 3. I will say the beginning sound and end sounds of a word:* /b/ /ōn/. *What word do you make when you blend these sounds together? Listen to these answer choices:* kite, bone, vase. *Circle the picture whose name blends the beginning and end sounds* /b/ /ōn/.

Phonemic Awareness

Turn to page 3, the page with a picture of a cat on it.

Check to see that all the children are on the correct page.

4 *Put your finger on the apple under the number 4. I will say three words:* rule, fume, huge. *Listen for the middle sound in each word:* /r/ /ū/ /l/, /f/ /ū/ /m/, /h/ /ū/ /j/. *Now listen to the answer choices:* hive, gate, dune. *Circle the picture whose name has the same middle sound you hear in* rule, fume, huge.

5 *Put your finger on the star under the number 5. I will say three words:* we, me, see. *Listen for the end sound in each word:* /w/ /ē/, /m/ /ē/, /s/ /ē/. *Now listen to the answer choices:* bee, tie, hay. *Circle the picture whose name has the same end sound you hear in* we, me, see.

6 *Put your finger on the tree under the number 6. I will say a word sound by sound:* /f/ /ē/ /t/. *What word do you make when you blend these sounds? Listen to these answer choices:* wave, feet, cube. *Circle the picture whose name you get when you blend the sounds:* /f/ /ē/ /t/.

Turn to page 4, the page with a picture of a dog on it.

Check to see that all the children are on the correct page.

7 *Put your finger on the apple under the number 7. I am going to say a word:* nose. *What new word do you make when you change the* /n/ *in* nose *to* /h/? *Listen to these answer choices:* queen, bike, hose. *Circle the picture that shows the new word you make when you change the* /n/ *in* nose *to* /h/.

8 *Put your finger on the star under the number 8. I will say a word:* tune. /tūūūnnn/. *How many sounds do you hear in the word* tune? *Circle the picture that shows how many sounds are in the word* tune.

Phonics

Turn to page 5, the page with a picture of an elephant on it.

Check to see that all the children are on the correct page.

9 *Put your finger on the apple under the number 9. Look at the picture. I will say the name of the picture:* pole. *Circle the word that names the picture.*

10 *Put your finger on the star under the number 10. Look at the picture. I will say the name of the picture:* cone. *Circle the word that names the picture.*

11 *Put your finger on the tree under the number 11 Look at the picture. I will say the name of the picture:* mule. *Circle the word that names the picture.*

Turn to page 6, the page with a picture of a frog on it.

Check to see that all the children are on the correct page.

12 *Put your finger on the apple under the number 12. Look at the picture. I will say the name of the picture:* tube. *Circle the word that names the picture.*

13 *Put your finger on the star under the number 13. Look at the picture. I will say the name of the picture:* peek. *Circle the word that names the picture.*

14 *Put your finger on the tree under the number 14. Look at the picture. I will say the name of the picture:* weed. *Circle the word that names the picture.*

High-Frequency Words

Turn to page 7, the page with a picture of a goat on it.
Check to see that all the children are on the correct page.

15 *Put your finger on the apple under the number 15. Listen to this sentence:* I know <u>where</u> my friend lives. *Read the answer choices. Circle the word* where.

16 *Put your finger on the star under the number 16. Listen to this sentence:* We can <u>look</u> for the lost toy. *Read the answer choices. Circle the word* look.

17 *Put your finger on the tree under the number 17. Listen to this sentence:* I will see <u>who</u> is knocking at the door. *Read the answer choices. Circle the word* who.

Turn to page 8, the page with a picture of a horse on it.

Check to see that all the children are on the correct page.

18 *Put your finger on the apple under the number 18. Listen to this sentence:* That is a <u>good</u> book. *Read the answer choices. Circle the word* good.

19 *Put your finger on the star under the number 19. Listen to this sentence:* His aunt will <u>come</u> for a visit. *Read the answer choices. Circle the word* come.

20 *Put your finger on the tree under the number 20. Listen to this sentence:* My dog <u>does</u> a trick. *Read the answer choices. Circle the word* does.

Unit Assessment · Unit 10 Teacher Script

Name: _____ Date: _____

UNITS 1–5 ASSESSMENT SCORING SHEET   UNIT ___

Item	Content Focus/CCSS	Score	Comments
Phonological Awareness			
1			
2			
3			
4			
Phonemic Awareness			
5			
6			
7			
8			
9			
10			
11			
Phonics			
12			
13			
14			
15			
16			
17			
High-Frequency Words			
18			
19			
20			

Name: _____ Date: _____

UNITS 6–10 ASSESSMENT SCORING SHEET   UNIT __

Item	Content Focus/CCSS	Score	Comments
Phonological Awareness			
1			
2			
3			
Phonemic Awareness			
4			
5			
6			
7			
8			
Phonics			
9			
10			
11			
12			
13			
14			
High-Frequency Words			
15			
16			
17			
18			
19			
20			

Assessment · Scoring Sheet

Unit Assessment Answer Key

UNIT 1

Question	Answer	Content Focus	CCSS
1	cap	Recognize Rhyme	RF.K.2a
2	bed	Recognize Rhyme	RF.K.2a
3	3 dots	Sentence Segmentation	RF.K.2
4	duck	Recognize Rhyme	RF.K.2a
5	2 dots	Sentence Segmentation	RF.K.2
6	4 dots	Sentence Segmentation	RF.K.2
7	top	Recognize Rhyme	RF.K.2a
8	2 dots	Recognize Syllables	RF.K.2b
9	net	Phoneme Isolation	RF.K.2d
10	sun	Phoneme Identity	RF.K.2d
11	fan	Phoneme Blending	RF.K.2b
12	A	Letter Recognition	RF.K.1d
13	m	Letter Recognition	RF.K.1d
14	m	Consonant *m*	RF.K.3a
15	m	Consonant *m*	RF.K.3a
16	a	Short *a*	RF.K.3b
17	a	Short *a*	RF.K.3b
18	I	High-Frequency Words	RF.K.3c
19	the	High-Frequency Words	RF.K.3c
20	we	High-Frequency Words	RF.K.3c

UNIT 2

Question	Answer	Content Focus	CCSS
1	mop	Onset/Rime Blending	RF.K.2c
2	pig	Onset/Rime Blending	RF.K.2c
3	sun	Recognize Alliteration	RF.K.2d
4	dog	Recognize Alliteration	RF.K.2d
5	nap	Phoneme Categorization	RF.K.2d
6	sock	Phoneme Categorization	RF.K.2d
7	jet	Phoneme Categorization	RF.K.2d
8	pen	Phoneme Blending	RF.K.2d
9	nut	Phoneme Blending	RF.K.2d
10	sad	Phoneme Isolation	RF.K.2d
11	log	Phoneme Isolation	RF.K.2d
12	sat	Consonant *s*	RF.K.3a
13	sap	Consonant *s*	RF.K.3a
14	pat	Consonant *p*	RF.K.3a
15	map	Consonant *p*	RF.K.3a
16	tap	Consonant *t*	RF.K.3a
17	mat	Consonant *t*	RF.K.3a
18	see	High-Frequency Words	RF.K.3c
19	a	High-Frequency Words	RF.K.3c
20	the	High-Frequency Words	RF.K.3c

Unit Assessment ·Answer Key

UNIT 3

Question	Answer	Content Focus	CCSS
1	I dot	Count and Pronounce Syllables	RF.K.2b
2	2 dots	Count and Pronounce Syllables	RF.K.2b
3	hill	Identify Rhyme	RF.K.2a
4	pin	Onset/Rime Blending	RF.K.2c
5	can	Phoneme Blending	RF.K.2d
6	soap	Phoneme Blending	RF.K.2d
7	2 dots	Phoneme Segmentation	RF.K.2d
8	3 dots	Phoneme Segmentation	RF.K.2d
9	comb	Phoneme Categorization	RF.K.2d
10	rug	Phoneme Categorization	RF.K.2d
11	seal	Phoneme Isolation	RF.K.2d
12	map	Consonant *m*	RF.K.3a
13	pat	Short *a*	RF.K.3b
14	sit	Short *i*	RF.K.3b
15	pin	Short *i*	RF.K.3b
16	nap	Consonant *n*	RF.K.3a
17	pan	Consonant *n*	RF.K.3a
18	like	High-Frequency Words	RF.K.3c
19	to	High-Frequency Words	RF.K.3c
20	and	High-Frequency Words	RF.K.3c

Unit Assessment · Answer Key

UNIT 4

Question	Answer	Content Focus	CCSS
1	2 dots	Count and Pronounce Syllables	RF.K.2b
2	1 dot	Count and Pronounce Syllables	RF.K.2b
3	3 dots	Count and Pronounce Syllables	RF.K.2b
4	4 dots	Sentence Segmentation	RF.K.2
5	deer	Phoneme Isolation	RF.K.2d
6	mop	Phoneme Isolation	RF.K.2d
7	fox	Phoneme Blending	RF.K.2d
8	cake	Phoneme Blending	RF.K.2d
9	2 dots	Phoneme Segmentation	RF.K.2d
10	3 dots	Phoneme Segmentation	RF.K.2d
11	pig	Phoneme Categorization	RF.K.2d
12	cap	Consonant c	RF.K.3a
13	cat	Consonant c	RF.K.3a
14	pot	Short o	RF.K.3b
15	top	Short o	RF.K.3b
16	dot	Consonant d	RF.K.3a
17	sad	Consonant d	RF.K.3a
18	go	High-Frequency Words	RF.K.3c
19	you	High-Frequency Words	RF.K.3c
20	do	High-Frequency Words	RF.K.3c

Unit Assessment · Answer Key

UNIT 5

Question	Answer	Content Focus	CCSS
1	cup	Recognize Rhyme	RF.K.2a
2	bat	Recognize Rhyme	RF.K.2a
3	2 dots	Count and Blend Syllables	RF.K.2b
4	web	Onset/Rime Blending	RF.K.2c
5	mouse	Phoneme Identity	RF.K.2d
6	dig	Phoneme Identity	RF.K.2d
7	bed	Phoneme Blending	RF.K.2d
8	hive	Phoneme Blending	RF.K.2d
9	3 dots	Phoneme Segmentation	RF.K.2d
10	nest	Phoneme Isolation	RF.K.2d
11	box	Phoneme Categorization	RF.K.2d
12	net	Consonant *n*	RF.K.3a
13	hit	Short *i*	RF.K.3b
14	hop	Consonant *h*	RF.K.3a
15	hat	Consonant *h*	RF.K.3a
16	pen	Short *e*	RF.K.3b
17	ten	Short *e*	RF.K.3b
18	and	High-Frequency Words	RF.K.3c
19	my	High-Frequency Words	RF.K.3c
20	are	High-Frequency Words	RF.K.3c

Unit Assessment • Answer Key

UNIT 6

Question	Answer	Content Focus	CCSS
1	hen	Recognize Rhyme	RF.K.2a
2	game	Recognize Rhyme	RF.K.2c
3	bug	Recognize Rhyme	RF.K.2a
4	bird	Phoneme Isolation	RF.K.2d
5	kite	Phoneme Isolation	RF.K.2d
6	robe	Phoneme Blending	RF.K.2d
7	leg	Phoneme Addition	RF.K.2e
8	3 dots	Phoneme Segmentation	RF.K.2d
9	fan	Consonant *f*	RF.K.3a
10	rip	Consonant *r*	RF.K.3a
11	bat	Consonant *b*	RF.K.3a
12	lip	Consonant *l*	RF.K.3a
13	kick	Consonant *k*	RF.K.3a
14	lock	Digraph *ck*	RF.K.3a
15	he	High-Frequency Words	RF.K.3c
16	with	High-Frequency Words	RF.K.3c
17	is	High-Frequency Words	RF.K.3c
18	little	High-Frequency Words	RF.K.3c
19	she	High-Frequency Words	RF.K.3c
20	was	High-Frequency Words	RF.K.3c

Unit Assessment · Answer Key

UNIT 7

Question	Answer	Content Focus	CCSS
1	wolf	Recognize Alliteration	RF.K.2d
2	goat	Onset/Rime Blending	RF.K.2c
3	dot	Recognize Rhyme	RF.K.2a
4	four	Phoneme Identity	RF.K.2d
5	den	Phoneme Blending	RF.K.2d
6	bus	Phoneme Addition	RF.K.2e
7	up	Phoneme Deletion	RF.K.2d
8	hen	Phoneme Substitution	RF.K.2e
9	bed	Short *e*	RF.K.3b
10	rug	Consonant *r*	RF.K.3a
11	kit	Consonant *k*	RF.K.3a
12	sun	Short *u*	RF.K.3b
13	log	Consonant *g*	RF.K.3a
14	wig	Consonant *w*	RF.K.3a
15	my	High-Frequency Words	RF.K.3c
16	was	High-Frequency Words	RF.K.3c
17	for	High-Frequency Words	RF.K.3c
18	have	High-Frequency Words	RF.K.3c
19	they	High-Frequency Words	RF.K.3c
20	of	High-Frequency Words	RF.K.3c

UNIT 8

Question	Answer	Content Focus	CCSS
1	jam	Onset/Rime Blending	RF.K.2c
2	van	Onset/Rime Blending	RF.K.2c
3	chick	Generate Rhyme	RF.K.2a
4	yarn	Phoneme Isolation	RF.K.2d
5	game	Phoneme Isolation	RF.K.2d
6	fox	Phoneme Blending	RF.K.2d
7	queen	Phoneme Substitution	RF.K.2e
8	4 dots	Phoneme Segmentation	RF.K.2d
9	six	Consonant *x*	RF.K.3a
10	vet	Consonant *v*	RF.K.3a
11	jog	Consonant *j*	RF.K.3a
12	quack	Consonant *qu*	RF.K.3a
13	yam	Consonant *y*	RF.K.3a
14	zip	Consonant *z*	RF.K.3a
15	said	High-Frequency Words	RF.K.3c
16	want	High-Frequency Words	RF.K.3c
17	here	High-Frequency Words	RF.K.3c
18	me	High-Frequency Words	RF.K.3c
19	this	High-Frequency Words	RF.K.3c
20	what	High-Frequency Words	RF.K.3c

Unit Assessment · Answer Key

UNIT 9

Question	Answer	Content Focus	CCSS
1	I dot	Syllable Segmentation	RF.K.2b
2	2 dots	Syllable Segmentation	RF.K.2b
3	hide	Generate Rhyme	RF.K.2a
4	mane	Phoneme Identity	RF.K.2d
5	wax	Phoneme Categorization	RF.K.2d
6	gate	Phoneme Addition	RF.K.2e
7	yolk	Phoneme Blending	RF.K.2d
8	ax	Phoneme Deletion	RF.K.2d
9	jug	Short *u*	RF.K.3b
10	van	Consonant *v*	RF.K.3a
11	wet	Consonant *w*	RF.K.3a
12	mix	Consonant *x*	RF.K.3a
13	wave	Long *a (a_e)*	RF.K.3b
14	dime	Long *i (i_e)*	RF.K.3b
15	want	High-Frequency Words	RF.K.3c
16	this	High-Frequency Words	RF.K.3c
17	help	High-Frequency Words	RF.K.3c
18	too	High-Frequency Words	RF.K.3c
19	play	High-Frequency Words	RF.K.3c
20	has	High-Frequency Words	RF.K.3c

UNIT 10

Question	Answer	Content Focus	CCSS
1	2 dots	Count and Blend Syllables	RF.K.2b
2	3 dots	Syllable Segmentation	RF.K.2b
3	bone	Onset/Rime Blending	RF.K.2c
4	dune	Phoneme Identity	RF.K.2d
5	bee	Phoneme Identity	RF.K.2d
6	feet	Phoneme Blending	RF.K.2d
7	hose	Phoneme Substitution	RF.K.2e
8	3 dots	Phoneme Segmentation	RF.K.2d
9	pole	Long o (o_e, o)	RF.K.3b
10	cone	Long o (o_e, o)	RF.K.3b
11	mule	Long u (u_e)	RF.K.3b
12	tube	Long *u* (u_e)	RF.K.3b
13	peek	Long e (ee, e_e, e)	RF.K.3b
14	weed	Long e (ee, e_e, e)	RF.K.3b
15	where	High-Frequency Words	RF.K.3c
16	look	High-Frequency Words	RF.K.3c
17	who	High-Frequency Words	RF.K.3c
18	good	High-Frequency Words	RF.K.3c
19	come	High-Frequency Words	RF.K.3c
20	does	High-Frequency Words	RF.K.3c

Unit Assessment · Answer Key

Diagnostic Assessments

Letter Naming and Sight Words

Name: _____ Date: _____

Record Sheet, Test 1

Letter Naming Fluency										# correct
g	H	t	X	r	F	C	j	T	z	__ /10
K	l	q	z	b	n	y	s	I	O	__ /10
A	e	V	u	Q	Y	z	M	j	a	__ /10
f	i	W	R	g	U	d	z	S	c	__ /10
k	M	g	D	o	J	n	p	m	h	__ /10
C	N	E	b	u	a	g	w	V	f	__ /10
G	Y	i	d	e	n	S	T	t	c	__ /10
R	F	a	m	Z	I	w	v	C	n	__ /10
f	s	P	o	Y	W	E	j	k	Q	__ /10
D	U	g	e	A	b	i	y	B	d	__ /10
N	f	p	R	F	q	l	K	p	M	__ /10
L	a	W	f	U	c	O	b	x	Z	__ /10

Total ____ /120

Assessment · Letter Naming Fluency

Letter Naming and Sight Words

Name: _____ **Date:** _____

Record Sheet, Test 2

Letter Naming Fluency										# correct
p	a	B	o	c	F	T	o	d	X	__ /10
D	p	M	i	G	j	b	h	b	z	__ /10
q	b	n	d	h	H	j	t	n	K	__ /10
R	y	b	c	e	U	e	X	a	r	__ /10
I	E	g	f	b	h	D	m	F	c	__ /10
y	F	m	s	a	Z	T	A	g	k	__ /10
i	W	J	Y	f	e	E	k	M	x	__ /10
A	g	S	c	h	R	I	j	V	f	__ /10
i	K	g	r	d	c	L	i	D	v	__ /10
J	t	e	C	k	N	h	G	l	Z	__ /10
V	g	H	F	j	f	C	I	e	u	__ /10
b	k	S	u	Y	B	l	d	L	Q	__ /10

Total ____ /120

Letter Naming and Sight Words

Name: _____ **Date:** _____

Record Sheet, Test 3

Letter Naming Fluency	# correct
a O q T v Q i e F n	__/10
u K g C b U o M F e	__/10
Z i u o J t h A p H	__/10
j B O c u b P q K e	__/10
w M a H A i r I d F	__/10
E t S i m f T C w a	__/10
r V D U I o s E Q e	__/10
o N r c q G M b Y r	__/10
t q L i B s d c H u	__/10
P i G f w g U k I Z	__/10
i l R y V g c I D v	__/10
S x a K s e L d R z	__/10

Total ____ /120

Assessment · Letter Naming Fluency

Letter Naming and Sight Words

Name: _____ Date: _____

Record Sheet, Test 4

Letter Naming Fluency										# correct
A	o	m	h	q	g	i	T	c	l	__ /10
f	c	n	F	R	e	j	s	R	t	__ /10
b	E	c	d	w	D	e	B	L	o	__ /10
d	K	e	S	a	Q	g	i	D	e	__ /10
f	C	j	c	V	a	G	b	I	g	__ /10
j	q	f	H	L	k	S	A	u	F	__ /10
Y	M	R	a	e	g	H	c	h	D	__ /10
w	u	B	z	J	l	g	K	h	__ /10
j	Q	d	b	o	U	x	N	m	B	__ /10
X	f	b	V	m	d	Z	x	C	h	__ /10
y	M	w	C	m	N	i	b	G	T	__ /10
f	b	O	g	A	f	P	i	q	W	__ /10

Total _____ /120

Letter Naming and Sight Words

Name: _____ Date: _____

Record Sheet, Test 5

Letter Naming Fluency	# correct
S E a T m D h I d U	__ /10
m D K X L f s a t r	__ /10
f j F e h n D L r K	__ /10
I A q S y i W U g e	__ /10
o n L d a j D F o P	__ /10
P b e V g O j I M T	__ /10
r T A S G n B d H o	__ /10
U d r M x e H z y e	__ /10
K U y j o T i c Y x	__ /10
F g i M b o L t H I	__ /10
z d S j y N k D m A	__ /10
R C o k f m b x y c	__ /10

Total ____ /120

Assessment · Letter Naming Fluency

Letter Naming and Sight Words

Name: _____ Date: _____

Record Sheet, Test 6

Letter Naming Fluency										# correct
A	G	X	i	r	e	s	D	P	u	__ /10
e	b	j	O	A	g	W	s	k	f	__ /10
Q	a	c	p	J	e	r	s	E	N	__ /10
i	F	H	d	p	m	T	h	j	P	__ /10
M	Z	t	n	S	Y	a	B	c	l	__ /10
o	X	u	K	T	i	U	o	b	J	__ /10
S	i	C	f	H	i	B	N	S	m	__ /10
g	m	g	e	K	f	l	w	d	M	__ /10
E	h	I	I	u	F	g	a	t	o	__ /10
W	q	O	k	f	L	R	q	M	r	__ /10
K	p	I	V	T	r	m	u	D	s	__ /10
r	V	d	C	G	s	L	y	v	p	__ /10

Total ___ /120

Letter Naming and Sight Words

Name: _____ **Date:** _____

Record Sheet, Test 7

Letter Naming Fluency	# correct
M x O P a g L q n j F	__ /10
s K h P d B a Z w c	__ /10
V b I u O T e G l J	__ /10
y R e Q i k H W a D	__ /10
I n F i p A e L P y	__ /10
w t B h R m U o l C	__ /10
N e W p v K L e M z	__ /10
f g D q S d Q i X Y	__ /10
O m P n R u e I Z o	__ /10
U y N b d K B o s l	__ /10
L E A j e q i u w I	__ /10
m n V b D F g j H k	__ /10

Total ___ /120

Assessment · Letter Naming Fluency

Letter Naming and Sight Words

Name: _____ Date: _____

Record Sheet, Test 8

Letter Naming Fluency										# correct
A	n	Q	v	C	B	h	P	j	r	__ /10
R	t	M	I	e	r	W	q	Z	o	__ /10
Q	w	N	h	f	H	A	D	a	S	__ /10
L	v	c	X	k	D	V	a	P	R	__ /10
O	I	g	u	e	b	G	k	u	Y	__ /10
d	u	B	I	A	m	n	V	p	U	__ /10
k	l	w	E	R	T	y	j	h	F	__ /10
O	x	t	v	N	B	o	a	E	r	__ /10
k	G	R	u	F	k	U	p	x	Z	__ /10
s	Q	L	i	b	V	C	m	N	t	__ /10
U	a	j	Q	y	l	A	o	i	p	__ /10
T	u	S	B	Z	a	q	e	E	W	__ /10

Total ____ /120

Letter Naming and Sight Words

Name: _____ Date: _____

Record Sheet, Test 9

Letter Naming Fluency										# correct
N	a	O	Q	v	C	U	X	z	I	__/10
M	j	I	g	A	H	r	t	u	S	__/10
R	T	u	Y	a	O	v	P	n	D	__/10
H	F	d	i	X	a	K	V	O	a	__/10
o	m	x	I	S	A	n	p	Q	c	__/10
K	j	n	C	w	i	m	z	D	p	__/10
W	o	P	z	q	L	x	j	t	K	__/10
V	B	n	V	y	o	u	A	L	N	__/10
I	K	Q	n	A	e	T	w	p	Y	__/10
a	b	V	H	B	t	d	C	R	m	__/10
C	u	q	b	E	f	y	S	n	G	__/10
z	A	c	U	n	A	s	E	F	t	__/10

Total ___ /120

Assessment · Letter Naming Fluency

Letter Naming and Sight Words

Name: _____ Date: _____

Record Sheet, Test 10

Letter Naming Fluency	# correct
Z m a K o R q v W A	___ /10
o P T d B i U y C s	___ /10
S y b L e f J M r d	___ /10
I e g Y u V w k T M	___ /10
R o D i M o E u Y G	___ /10
n Q B n x l K P b S	___ /10
L e a S i A v k J I	___ /10
J s A T h i Z o P F	___ /10
y D f P u B y Z S x	___ /10
W c Q n o r M v H E	___ /10
N a s R K y C T g Z	___ /10
G N x v i A I m E t	___ /10

Total ___ /120

Letter Naming and Sight Words

Name: _____ Date: _____

Record Sheet, Test 1

Sight Word Fluency					# of errors
and	are	do	for	go	__ /5
has	is	she	here	of	__ /5
see	who	look	said	my	__ /5
play	like	see	he	want	__ /5
the	what	help	good	this	__ /5
out	run	new	live	her	__ /5
some	grow	none	fall	carry	__ /5
food	build	give	ago	eat	__ /5
oh	sure	four	near	woman	__ /5
gone	learn	know	write	push	__ /5
through	guess	surprise	above	children	__ /5
thought	laugh	round	climb	heard	__ /5

Total number of words read in one minute	
Number of errors	
Accuracy rate (use Oral Reading Accuracy formula)	

Assessment · Sight Word Fluency

Letter Naming and Sight Words

Name: _____ Date: _____

Record Sheet, Test 2

Sight Word Fluency					# of errors
go	and	for	come	do	__ /5
does	me	can	here	are	__ /5
we	to	you	is	of	__ /5
help	look	have	with	the	__ /5
he	they	what	too	play	__ /5
be	not	up	fun	move	__ /5
no	call	so	or	were	__ /5
soon	done	upon	our	full	__ /5
door	warm	after	early	old	__ /5
water	nothing	knew	animal	blue	__ /5
again	many	school	could	three	__ /5
caught	favorite	front	people	work	__ /5

Total number of words read in one minute	
Number of errors	
Accuracy rate (use Oral Reading Accuracy formula)	

Letter Naming and Sight Words

Name: _____ Date: _____

Record Sheet, Test 3

Sight Word Fluency					# of errors
is	has	see	here	me	__ /5
to	was	she	of	does	__ /5
this	they	want	my	with	__ /5
good	said	who	where	have	__ /5
little	play	go	like	can	__ /5
one	day	more	ate	few	__ /5
two	by	they	over	use	__ /5
very	began	another	then	jump	__ /5
love	been	eyes	only	great	__ /5
enough	brother	over	more	father	__ /5
toward	push	brought	wonder	grow	__ /5
walk	poor	because	picture	large	__ /5

Total number of words read in one minute	
Number of errors	
Accuracy rate (use Oral Reading Accuracy formula)	

Assessment · Sight Word Fluency

Letter Naming and Sight Words

Name: _____ **Date:** _____

Record Sheet, Test 4

Sight Word Fluency					# of errors
to	and	the	he	was	__ /5
have	me	we	she	come	__ /5
see	look	said	with	of	__ /5
like	who	too	where	are	__ /5
they	for	what	you	does	__ /5
am	any	boy	from	into	__ /5
happy	flew	well	fun	new	__ /5
put	pretty	why	other	green	__ /5
brown	poor	color	right	found	__ /5
friend	should	would	about	small	__ /5
year	month	money	young	away	__ /5
picture	question	instead	brother	busy	__ /5

Total number of words read in one minute	
Number of errors	
Accuracy rate (use Oral Reading Accuracy formula)	

Letter Naming and Sight Words

Name: _____ Date: _____

Record Sheet, Test 5

Sight Word Fluency					# of errors
is	he	can	we	are	__ /5
my	for	do	come	me	__ /5
see	too	said	look	want	__ /5
where	you	play	little	help	__ /5
does	have	good	this	has	__ /5
but	yes	say	way	find	__ /5
make	start	small	yellow	eight	__ /5
around	funny	under	black	again	__ /5
year	their	once	young	better	__ /5
your	mother	their	because	love	__ /5
month	surprise	another	friend	eyes	__ /5
enough	tomorrow	listen	children	busy	__ /5

Total number of words read in one minute	
Number of errors	
Accuracy rate (use Oral Reading Accuracy formula)	

Assessment · Sight Word Fluency